Dawkins and the Selfish Gene

Ed Sexton

Series editor: Richard Appignanesi

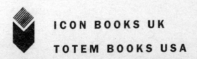

ICON BOOKS UK

TOTEM BOOKS USA

Published in the UK in 2001
by Icon Books Ltd., Grange Road,
Duxford, Cambridge CB2 4QF
E-mail: info@iconbooks.co.uk
www.iconbooks.co.uk

Published in the USA in 2001
by Totem Books
Inquiries to: Icon Books Ltd.,
Grange Road, Duxford,
Cambridge CB2 4QF, UK

Sold in the UK, Europe, South Africa
and Asia by Faber and Faber Ltd.,
3 Queen Square, London WC1N 3AU
or their agents

Distributed to the trade in the USA by
National Book Network Inc.,
4720 Boston Way, Lanham,
Maryland 20706

Distributed in the UK, Europe,
South Africa and Asia by
Macmillan Distribution Ltd.,
Houndmills, Basingstoke RG21 6XS

Distributed in Canada by
Penguin Books Canada,
10 Alcorn Avenue, Suite 300,
Toronto, Ontario M4V 3B2

Published in Australia in 2001
by Allen & Unwin Pty. Ltd.,
83 Alexander Street,
Crows Nest, NSW 2065

Library of Congress catalog
card number applied for

Text copyright © 2001 Ed Sexton

The author has asserted his moral rights.

Series editor: Richard Appignanesi

ISBN 1 84046 238 8

Typesetting by Wayzgoose

Printed and bound in the UK by
Cox & Wyman Ltd., Reading

Introduction

[M]an's way of life is largely determined by culture rather than by genes.[1]

This is perhaps not a quotation we would normally associate with Richard Dawkins. It does, however, exemplify two points which I hope to make in this book. I hope to show that much of Dawkins' 'selfish gene' theory has been misinterpreted, and that therefore much of the criticism he has received is misdirected. A few well-chosen quotations can be highly misleading and can bury the meaning of any complex theory, which brings me to the second point: many (but by no means all) of Dawkins' critics focus on his rhetoric, rather than the theory he describes.

Of course, the rhetoric of *The Selfish Gene* is all too easy to criticise. Dawkins' metaphorical and often aggressive use of language can alienate readers rather than persuade them. Certain words are downright confusing, such as 'selfish' in the title, which the author constantly reminds us he is using in a 'special' way. Putting aside our common understanding of these words and replacing them with Dawkinspeak is not helped by the occasional outbursts and anti-religious swipes which litter the book, a point emphasised by Merryl Wyn Davies:

Dawkins may maintain he believes that genes make us but do not compel us, yet his 'giddying updraughts of rhetoric' are repeatedly and passionately defended by their author; they persuasively convey meaning.[2]

This is not to say that there aren't real objections to selfish gene theory. Philosophers and scientists alike have criticised Dawkins for ignoring various aspects of evolution, for advocating a form of genetic determinism, for reducing all social behaviour to the behaviour of genes, and so on. Perhaps the most popular criticism is that selfish gene theory somehow undermines religion and morality. The 'somehow' in that sentence will no doubt tell readers that I think this last objection is unfounded. Theories about facts, while undoubtedly informing moral and social debate, cannot serve as a basis for morality. Or, more succinctly, 'you can't get an ought from an is'.[3]

There is a problem, of course, if religion claims something factual which contradicts a scientific theory. Thus, creationists seem to be locked into an endless battle with evolutionists, a topic reviewed in Merryl Wyn Davies' *Darwin and Fundamentalism*, another volume in this series.[4] *Dawkins and the Selfish Gene* is not about the arguments for and against evolutionary theory in general. Many evolutionary biologists disagree with selfish gene theory, and those who reject evolutionary theory itself inevitably reject Dawkins' work. Theirs is an argument concerning the facts of life's history – Dawkins' theory concerns the mechanisms behind those facts, if the basic tenets of evolution are true.

You may feel that the first page of *The Selfish Gene* suggests otherwise. Consider the following rhetoric:

We no longer have to resort to superstition when faced with the deep problems: Is there a meaning to life? What are we for? What is man?[5]

Dawkins' atheism is waved proudly here and elsewhere, but it would be wrong to say that selfish gene theory is in itself opposed to all religious points of view. It may tell us what we are for in the sense of what evolution has constructed us to do, but it certainly doesn't tell us how to live our lives as conscious human beings.

When it was first published in 1976, *The Selfish Gene* was a straightforward science book. It was based on the principles of neo-Darwinism, which reconciled the relatively new field of genetics with Darwin's insights into evolution by natural selection. Darwin's theory had shown how organisms could evolve if the hereditary factors passed down by each generation were open to mutation. Some of these mutations would be advantageous, in the sense that they would increase the organism's chances of surviving and passing on the mutations (for example, faster running ability). Many would be extremely disadvantageous (for example, one leg). Thus, in a sense, nature would select those individuals most able to survive, who would pass on the mutated hereditary factors (with some new mutations), and so on – evolution by natural selection. Darwin had little idea what these hereditary factors were, or how they could mutate and be passed down the generations. Today we know them by the all-too-familiar word 'gene'.

Dawkins took this new way of thinking about evolution and applied it to one specific area. It was not to be a grand new theory. Instead,

. . . it will explore the consequences of the evolution theory for a particular issue. My purpose is to examine the biology of selfishness and altruism.[6]

On the way, however, Dawkins developed a new 'gene centred' way of looking at evolution and biology which laid bare the fallacy in 'good of the species' or even 'good of the individual' arguments. If there was good to be had, it was by the gene. Dawkins' theory was not merely confined to genes – it could be applied to any system of replicating entities which undergo mutation and selection. Artificial Life research has felt its implications, and the last chapter of *The Selfish Gene* even suggests that thoughts could be evolving – the infamous 'memes'.

Meanwhile, as the book's popularity increased, so did the controversy. Religious and philosophical objections started to appear, fuelled by the media, which only helped to raise Dawkins' fame. For some, he was – and remains – a devoted and passionate scientist at the forefront of evolutionary theory; for others, he is still the embodiment of the threat that science poses to social values.

At the very end of the 1989 edition of *The Selfish Gene*, Dawkins summarises the entire selfish gene theory, with additions from *The Extended Phenotype* published in 1982.[7] Before examining the issues in detail, a brief summary of that summary may be useful.

Selfish genes in a nutshell

The fundamental unit of evolution is the replicator. A replicator is anything which can be copied under certain circumstances; so, in a sense, a salt crystal could be a replicator. Unlike salt crystals, however, there is a small error when replicators are copied, so the population of replicators shows variety and changes over time. Suppose a sculptor is asked to copy a famous sculpture. He will undoubtedly not reproduce it exactly, and any subsequent copies of the sculptor's reproduction will 'inherit' these small changes. At the same time, other copies will have different mistakes in them, which will also be handed down.

How well all of these non-identical copies will fare depends on the conditions they're in – their environment. Firstly, what do we mean when we say 'how well a replicator does'? We simply mean how well it continues to replicate; how many new replicators it gives rise to. Evolution knows no other criterion for success. Most mutations will have devastating results, destroying the replicator's capacity to be copied. In our imperfect sculpture analogy, this could correspond to a copy which is so distorted that no future artists will want to copy it. Some mutations, however, will increase the replicator's chances of replicating. Some mutations will confer benefits on the replicator to help it succeed at the expense of other replicators. These replicators will produce new copies which will inherit the mutation, while their less successful brethren will be consigned to history. Thus, we have a natural selection of those replicators most able to succeed, leading to the evolution of new replicator properties.

Some replicators will benefit from working together. Suppose replicator A has evolved the ability to copy itself in a new world record time, but only in the presence of a certain substance, say salt. Replicator B, meanwhile, has a mutation which means it attracts dissolved salt, but lacks any special copying ability. Apart, they fare no better or worse than their peers, but together they will proliferate in the replicator population. Over time, evolution will ensure that they are copied together, probably via further mutations physically linking them.

This population of replicators working together for mutual benefit may, in time, give rise to 'vehicles': physical entities in which many replicators co-exist. A vehicle is designed and built by the combined action of the replicators inside it, and successful vehicles will be those which manage to copy their replicators (and hence the vehicle). Thus, the population of vehicles will give rise to new generations of vehicles, all inheriting the same replicators. Mutations will continue to occur, and replicators will evolve more and more elaborate vehicles in their quest to out-compete their peers. They may evolve the ability to destroy other vehicles and utilise the materials they are composed of. They may even evolve the ability to manipulate the behaviour of other vehicles to their own advantage. These replicators are locked in an evolutionary arms race – whoever builds the most successful vehicle wins.

I have tried to avoid calling replicators 'selfish', or implying purpose, because the process is blind. There is no conscious attempt by replicators to out-wit their fellows. It is simply the case that those which do in fact 'selfishly' exploit other replicators will tend to be copied more, and more copies of them will be present in the next generation.

In biological evolution, the replicators are genes and the vehicles are organisms, like us. It is possible that genes could have stayed floating around in the seas – there is nothing inevitable in the creation of vehicles, as Dawkins points out at the end of the 1989 edition:

11

[T]*he individual body, so familiar to us on our planet, did not have to exist. The only kind of entity that has to exist in order for life to arise . . . is the immortal replicator.*[8]

Immortal because, although vehicles are designed, built, and eventually degrade, replicators march through the generations, albeit as copies. Strictly, the mutations introduced into each new generation mean that most replicators will eventually be changed beyond recognition, but this process is slow compared to the working life of a vehicle. Human genes have taken many millions of years to evolve – some genes in you have remained almost unchanged for hundreds of millions of years – but if the Bible is to be believed, the human vehicle lasts just three score years and ten. We can now see why Dawkins called his book *The Selfish Gene*, even though 'The self-perpetuating replicator, which appears to act selfishly due to the operation of natural selection, but has in fact no conscious foresight whatsoever' may have been a more precise title. Oxford University Press probably wouldn't have sold many copies with that.

We have looked at replicators and vehicles, which in the natural world correspond to genes and organisms. We have seen that an organism is a vehicle for its genes – it exists because of them, it was designed by them, and its 'purpose' is to get them copied by whatever means necessary. So let us now turn to two important questions: what exactly is a gene, and what happens when we apply Dawkins' theory of genes as replicators to the biological world?

A gene by any other name . . .

Pinning down exactly what a gene is turns out to be no easy task. A geneticist may define it as 'the basic unit of heredity', a molecular biologist as 'a peptide-encoding length of DNA'. Dawkins defines it as 'the fundamental unit of natural selection', i.e., the replicator responsible for evolution on earth.[9]

A quick review of the biology involved may clarify the issue. All, or almost all, life on earth is built on DNA.[10] DNA is a long but simple molecule, consisting of regularly repeating sub-units which encode the genetic information. Just as a computer disk is essentially a long series of data split into different files, so a single DNA molecule may have many functional genes encoded along its length. Unlike the binary system of computers, however, in which every 'bit' of data is represented by a 0 or a 1, DNA uses four different chemical compounds, called nucleotides. These are usually written A, T, C and G, using the first letters of their chemical names. If you 'read' the sequence on a computer disk, you may get '10001001110', whereas a DNA sequence would look like 'ATTCGATTCG'. When DNA is sequenced, the result is a gel with four columns marked in correspondence to the four 'letters' of DNA's alphabet. Distance along the DNA molecule is represented vertically, and horizontal lines in each column show which letter is at that position. I mention this only because it is one of the media's stock images when discussing the matter.

In general, the information encoded by DNA is used for making one thing: proteins.[11] These proteins not only make up the organic structures of which you and I are composed, they also regulate in precise detail the workings of the cell, and hence the organism. They control chemical reactions responsible for everything from digesting your food to repairing damaged skin. It is through proteins that DNA makes its mark on the world. Change the DNA sequence and you change the protein sequence, thus the effect it has on the organism. 'Start' and 'stop' signals ensure that the cell 'knows' where protein-encoding regions begin and end – molecular biologists call this functional unit a 'cistron' to avoid the problems of the ill-defined gene. To distinguish between the information carried on DNA and its effects, biologists use the terms 'genotype' and 'phenotype'. Suppose you carry a gene for blue eyes: your genotype describes the DNA involved, while the phenotype (the gene's effects) is 'blue eyes'.[12] The complete genotype of an organism – i.e., all its genes – is called its 'genome'. In many organisms, the genome is split between several long DNA molecules – 'chromosomes'. In our computer analogy, this corresponds to having several disks of data.

Humans have 23 pairs of chromosomes, in

which each pair functions as duplicates. Suppose our eye pigment gene is located at a certain position on chromosome 3. This means that there will be a gene for eye pigment at the same position on both copies of chromosome 3. However, the exact DNA sequence may differ between the copies – one may encode a blue pigment, the other a green pigment. These variations are called 'alleles'. So the gene for eye pigment may possess a 'blue' allele, a 'green' allele, and so on. Usually alleles differ from each other by just a few nucleotides. Whether the individual ends up with blue eyes, green eyes or something in between, depends on the gene, and alleles, involved. In actual human eye colour, the brown allele is 'dominant' to blue – so an individual with one copy of the blue gene and one copy of the brown will have brown eyes. Blue is then said to be 'recessive' to brown. An individual with two blue alleles would, of course, have blue eyes. The relationship between other pigment combinations is somewhat more complicated. In computer terminology, this system is equivalent to having two of each disk, where the same files are present on each copy in the same place. The exact content of the files, however, may differ by small amounts.

Eggs and sperm (sex cells) contain just one of each pair of chromosomes, and thus just one of the two possible alleles. These combine with your partner's sex cells after fertilisation to produce the full complement of 23 pairs, and hence a new genome – your offspring's. The only slight oddity is the sex chromosomes, called X and Y. Although a woman's two X chromosomes form a matching pair, the XY combination in men doesn't. The Y chromosome is significantly smaller than the X chromosome, and thus lacks a large portion of its genes. They separate in the usual way when sex cells are formed – which means that sex is determined by the male's genes: an egg must contain an X chromosome, whereas a sperm can contain either an X or a Y.

The last complication in the process is that, before the chromosomes are bundled off into sex cells, DNA can be 'swapped' between the pairs in a process called 'crossing-over'. So instead of giving your offspring one or other chromosome, you may pass on a chromosome composed one third of one copy and two thirds of the other, for example. In our disk analogy, this is equivalent to swapping some of the files on one disk with the corresponding files on the other. In this way, two new disks have been created, composed of parts of the former pair. In most species, which parts of the chromosomes cross over is fairly random, so a new unique chromosome tends to be produced each time. Of course, if the chromosomes in the original pair were identical (i.e., they had the same alleles for each gene on the chromosome), crossing-over would produce no net change! In practice, however, there will be differences at many gene locations. Thus, each sex cell will inherit a unique set of 23 chromosomes.

Armed with this knowledge of molecular genetics, we can now make sense of the definitions of a gene. To most biologists, the gene is a functional piece of DNA which encodes one protein (roughly the sense in which I have been using it until now): a cistron. Dawkins, however, adapts George Williams' definition and sees a gene as:

. . . *any portion of chromosomal material that*

potentially lasts for enough generations to serve
as a unit of natural selection.[13]

We have seen that replicators must persist (albeit as copies) for many generations, if they are to act as a target for natural selection. Thus, chromosomes themselves cannot be replicators – they are chopped up and reformed in each generation, thanks to crossing-over. Parts of chromosomes may not necessarily be destroyed in this way – they may survive many generations before being split. As the process is more or less random, the smaller the length of chromosome, the less likely it is that it will be destroyed, and the more generations we can expect it to survive intact.

This is the first problem. For crossing-over does not respect the boundaries of cistrons – bits of files can be swapped with corresponding bits on the other disk. Thus, eventually, we should expect any length of 'chromosomal material', no matter how small it is, to be split in two, never again to meet. Even a single pair of nucleotides will eventually part company. This point is made by Mark Ridley:

[I]*f we take a long enough view, the only finally permanent units in the genome are nucleotide bases . . . However, this long view holds little interest for us, as we are concerned with the time scale of natural selection. It takes a thousand or so generations for a mutation's frequency to be significantly altered and, over this time, genes, but not genomes or phenotypes, will be practically unaltered.*[14]

This is why Dawkins uses the phrase 'enough generations' in his definition. The gene is that part of a chromosome which persists unaltered *long enough* for selection to influence its frequency. So, of course, the gene is the unit of selection – it is defined to be exactly that!

A gene is thus a vague entity. We cannot easily identify a piece of chromosome as being a gene in Dawkins' sense unless it has proved its persistence over time. Some 'genes' may in fact consist of many sequential cistrons. Later, we will examine whether or not selection acts just at this genetic level. Are individuals, groups or species possible targets for selection? Are they true replicators? If we find that they are, perhaps we would be tempted to call them genes! Dawkins is clear, however, that while he does not pretend to have a precise physical definition of the gene, it is a length of DNA lying somewhere between the cistron and the chromosome. Ridley again summarises the point:

Williams defined the gene . . . as 'that which segregates and recombines with appreciable frequency'. According to this definition, the gene need not be the same as a cistron . . . Rather, it is the length of chromosome that has sufficient permanence for natural selection to adjust its frequency . . . In practice, the replicator (or Williams' gene) does not consistently correspond to any particular length of DNA.[15]

Selfishness and altruism

We can now see what it means to talk of 'selfish genes'. It doesn't mean that genes are devious, self-interested bits of DNA, hell-bent on manipulating their environment to their advantage. It simply means that those genes which affect their

21

environment in such a way that they proliferate, often at the expense of other ('rival') genes, will – well, proliferate. 'Nice' genes that help their competitors at their own expense will die out. That's all there is to it.

Given that in most circumstances all genes in an organism share a common method of proliferating, via reproduction, we will expect organisms to act in such a way as to maximise their own chances of reproducing, often at the expense of others. Furthermore, 'others' in this context is not just other species – it includes members of the same species, even members of the same group. In fact, we might expect organisms to behave more selfishly in their dealings with their own species, since these are the individuals they are competing against for resources such as food, shelter or mates. There are countless examples of such selfish behaviour. I will mention just one:

. . . male lions, who, when newly arrived in a pride, sometimes murder existing cubs, presumably because these are not their own children.[16]

So much for animals acting for the good of the species.

However, remember that it is the genes that are calling the shots here, not the organism. If genes cared about anything, which obviously they don't, it certainly wouldn't be the organism. The organism is merely a vehicle – genes' method of copying themselves. There are numerous situations in which genes' interest is best served not by having the organism stubbornly competing against other individuals, but by co-operating or even helping them. Which raises the flip side of the selfishness coin – altruism.

Strictly speaking, altruism refers to behaviour which lowers the altruistic individual's chances of reproducing, while increasing the chances of the lucky recipient. The term is also used in situations where there is no obvious harm done to the altruist – pedants who need to justify the strict meaning can view energy and time costs as the 'harm done'. Organisms clearly are altruistic in this sense – think of the efforts that parents make to protect their children – but why?

The problem evaporates when we remind ourselves that it is genes that matter, not individuals. From the genes' point of view, it is obvious that parents should take risks in protecting their children, because those children are the vehicle which will carry them through another generation. For some reason, people see the parent–child relationship as somehow different, as something that does not need explanation. Yet those same people demand an explanation for altruism between other relatives, and between individuals not obviously related at all. Keeping to relatives for the moment, we can see that from the genes' point of view there is no difference between the mother–child relationship and the brother–sister relationship – in both cases, the chances of a gene which is present in one being present in the other is 50 per cent:

We can now see that parental care is just a special case of kin altruism. Genetically speaking, an adult should devote just as much care and attention to its orphaned baby brother as it does to one of its own children ... In practice ... brotherly or sisterly care is nothing like so common in nature as parental care.[17]

One reason why parental care is so much more common is that, while in terms of their relatedness to you, your children and siblings may be identical, in practice there are important differences between them. For example, your children will probably have more of their reproductive lives ahead of them than your siblings, and thus represent a better investment (in gene terms). Similarly, we should expect individuals to show altruism towards other relatives in proportion to their relatedness to them, subject to a variety of conditions of which reproductive expectancy is just one. This explanation of kin altruism is often called 'kin selection', and was elegantly described in mathematical terms by William Hamilton in 1964.[18] Of course, the genes are not behaving altruistically – they are merely helping other vehicles which are likely to contain copies of themselves.

Some may immediately see a defence of 'the good of the species' argument hidden in here. Surely, they cry, given that all members of a species share a very large number of genes, we should expect this kin altruism to extend to all the organism's peers? After all, in some sense, they are all relatives. One response is that it is a case of diminishing returns. If your sister needs half of your supper to survive, it may be worth you sharing – there is only a small chance that you will suffer malnourishment, and she is highly related to you. If it's your third cousin once removed, however, you will still have to expend the same effort and take the same risks to help him, but the benefit is greatly reduced, as he is a fairly distant relative. An organism only has so much time and energy, and there will come a point when it simply will not be worth it – as far as propagating genes is concerned, anyway.

Another issue is the problem of estimating your relatedness to the prospective beneficiary. If you are going to make a judgement about whether or not to help an individual, you must know how closely related you are to him or her – i.e., what the chances are of you sharing any one particular gene. Since animals clearly do not engage in complex mathematical calculations, there are more direct rules to judge your relatedness to someone, such as physical likeness. You can probably see family resemblances in most of your close relatives. The further you move away through the family tree, the harder this process becomes. While you may be able to judge that your brother looks more like you than your cousin, telling your third cousin from your fourth could prove tricky.

This does mean, of course, that we may expect animals which live in extended family groups generally to behave altruistically to other members of the group. Some would claim that this is a form of group selection ('the good of the group' argument), and indeed it may look that way at first. However, it is genes that are being selected, and the epiphenomenon (side-effect) of the group behaving as a co-operative unit only results from the fact that the group members are reasonably close relatives. If the group was regularly infiltrated by non-relatives, the behaviour would never have evolved, or at least group members would develop a method of discriminating between their true relatives and the impostors.

Yet altruism also occurs between organisms that have no obvious relation to each other, or no obvious way of knowing whether or not they are related. Birds shout warning calls when they spot predators, monkeys groom each other, and so on. How can selfish gene theory possibly explain these cases? The answer is reciprocal altruism – the idea that 'if you scratch my back, I'll scratch yours'.

Dawkins succinctly outlines the condition necessary for reciprocal altruism to occur:

If animals live together in groups their genes must get more benefit out of the association than they put in.

He goes on to list some examples:

A pack of hyenas can catch prey so much larger than a lone hyena can bring down that it pays each selfish individual to hunt in a pack, even though this involves sharing food. It is probably for similar reasons that some spiders co-operate in building a huge communal web. Emperor penguins conserve heat by huddling together.[19]

Incidentally, this last example is related to a more general explanation of 'bunching behaviour' in animals. Many animals, particularly grazing herbivores, seem to have a gregarious nature. Dawkins summarises Hamilton's theory that bunching behaviour is the product of a selection pressure from predators. The idea is that each grazing animal obviously does not want to be the nearest to any predators in the area. How can it achieve this? By surrounding itself with other members of the group – that way they are more likely to be eaten! Unfortunately, everyone wants the same thing, and in a real herd someone will have to be on the outside. Hence:

[T]*here will be a ceaseless migration in from the edges of an aggregation towards the centre. If the herd was previously loose and straggling, it will soon become tightly bunched as a result of the inward migration. Even if we start our model with no tendency towards aggregation at all, and the . . . animals start by being randomly dispersed, the selfish urge of each individual will be to reduce his domain of danger by trying to position himself in a gap between other individuals.*[20]

As Dawkins points out, there is no reciprocal

altruism involved here. The physical closeness of the individuals does not imply any co-operative behaviour – merely that there is a good (selfish) reason for being physically close. Surely the huddling behaviour of penguins is similar, in that it is presumably colder at the edges of a huddle than at the centre?

Yet we still have to explain behaviour which exhibits true reciprocal altruism. Under what conditions will animals co-operate – when will genes 'get more benefit out of the association than they put in'? The well-known prisoner's dilemma, the basis of much game theory, provides an answer.

The original form of the dilemma went something like this. You are one of two prisoners charged with a heinous crime. If both of you confess to the crime, you will each receive ten years. However, if you confess and your 'partner' doesn't, you will get off with just six months, and he will go down for 20 years. At this stage, confessing looks sensible – after all, if your partner does and you don't, you'll get 20 years, when you could have reduced it to ten. If he's a true friend and keeps his mouth shut, you can be out in six months by betraying him! But what happens if both of you refuse to talk? In this dilemma, mutual co-operation has a benefit, because there's only enough evidence to imprison each of you for a year. But if you are interrogated separately, you will not be able to reach this agreement – there's no way to be sure your partner won't confess and stick you behind bars for 20 years. Whatever your partner does, you're better off confessing – either you'll get six months instead of a year, or ten years instead of 20. As both of you are thinking like this, you both confess and end up with ten years. And to think you could have been out in one . . .

The dilemma comes from the problem of not being able to trust your partner. If you've been in similar situations with him before, however, you will presumably have developed a trusting friendship, and will hence co-operate to get a one-year sentence. This is the key: while confessing (defecting) is the only sensible (selfish) strategy in a one-off prisoner's dilemma, in a repeated encounter it is possible to take previous behaviour into account. So which strategy is most effective in a repeated prisoner's dilemma? Should prisoners always co-operate, or perhaps cheat on each other occasionally? If so, how often?

Dawkins discusses the work of Robert Axelrod, who set out to find the best strategy in a prisoner's dilemma using computer modelling. On a computer, many different strategies can be rapidly played off against each other over hundreds of encounters, with scores corresponding to prison sentences. Despite many deviously complicated strategies, to this day the most successful remains one of the simplest, called Tit-for-Tat.[21] Tit-for-Tat starts off by being nice and co-operating. After that, it simply copies its opponent (or partner, depending on how you look at it). So if it is cheated on the first round, it will retaliate on the second round. This may lead to both sides retaliating endlessly, but at least Tit-for-Tat will have suffered the '20 year' penalty only once, at the start. If it meets nice strategies that don't cheat, a never-ending period of harmonious co-operation will result.

So how does this relate to the evolution of altruistic behaviour? Prisoners' dilemmas abound in nature. The 'you scratch my back, I'll scratch yours' scenario is repeated in countless forms in animal interactions. Should I cheat and not scratch your back? In this example, there is a delay between paying the cost and receiving the benefit, but the overall situation mirrors the prisoner's dilemma.

In nature, of course, the rewards aren't measured in terms of scores or reduced prison sentences – they're handed out as offspring. So a behaviour which is successful at repeated 'prisoners' dilemmas' will tend to spread in the population. This is especially good news for Tit-for-Tat, as we have seen that it performs best when it encounters other Tit-for-Tattists. Note that a saintly strategy which was always nice, whatever its opponent did, would do just as well in this scenario. In fact, it would be impossible to tell apart a population of saints and a group of Tit-for-Tattists. But there is one important difference. While the Tit-for-Tattists will weed out any cheats that infiltrate the group by retaliating against them, the saints can be exploited to extinction by such cheats.[22] And natural selection based on mutation ensures that there will always be selfish cheats popping up to take advantage of any suckers out there.

In some sense, Tit-for-Tat is a more stable strategy – it is less open to invasion from other strategies. Dawkins follows Maynard Smith in referring to it as an evolutionarily stable strategy, or ESS. An ESS is:

. . . a strategy which, if most members of a population adopt it, cannot be bettered by an alternative strategy.[23]

Or, as he rephrases it in the 1989 edition:

. . . a strategy that does well against copies of itself.[24]

Theory does in fact suggest that a population of Tit-for-Tat can be invaded to a small degree by other strategies, so we might want to say that some mixture of strategies, mostly Tit-for-Tat, is an ESS. The other strategies will be partly saints who will be exploited by some cheats, so the population ends up reflecting a spectrum from 'saint' to 'cheat', with the 'you scratch my back, I'll scratch yours' mentality dominating. As Dawkins comments:

Some might see this as a mirror for familiar aspects of human life.[25]

Necessarily brief as this explanation of reciprocal altruism has been, I hope it convinces the reader that it is perfectly possible, and indeed likely, that genes for such behaviour will evolve under natural selection and in accordance with selfish gene theory. There are some times when it simply pays to co-operate, no matter how selfish you are.

There is plenty more that can be said, by way of example and application of theory, to explain and illustrate Dawkins' selfish gene theory. Before moving onto criticisms and problems with Dawkins' view, I will conclude with an outline of three of the many areas to which Dawkins applies his theory: symbiosis, deciding when to have children, and the problem of the opposite sex.

Symbiosis

We usually talk about reciprocal altruism between members of the same species. There is no reason why such relationships cannot exist between members of different species. Feeding aphids produce a sugar-rich 'honeydew' which forms as droplets on their back ends. Some species of ant 'milk' the aphids by stroking their hindquarters and eating the resulting honeydew, and there is evidence that the aphids go out of their way to make this easy for the ants. In return for this supply of food, the aphids receive protection from predators. In some examples of this phenomenon, ants actually incubate the aphid eggs in their own nests, feed the young insects and then carry the adults up to feeding points in the plant. Dawkins explains the relationship:

Aphids have the right sort of mouthparts for pumping up plant sap, but such sucking mouthparts are no good for self-defence. Ants are no good at sucking sap from plants, but they are good at fighting. Ant genes for cultivating and protecting aphids have been favoured in ant gene-pools. Aphid genes for co-operating with the ants have been favoured in aphid gene-pools.[26]

Such relationships can evolve, in accordance with selfish gene theory, and become the norm between two species:

A relationship of mutual benefit between members of different species is called mutualism or symbiosis. Members of different species often have much to offer each other because they can bring different 'skills' to the partnership. This kind of fundamental asymmetry can lead to evolutionarily stable strategies of mutual cooperation.[27]

In some circumstances, the relationship can become so intimate that it is difficult to tell the two species apart. For example, familiar lichens are in fact composed of two species, one a fungus and the other a green alga. The two species have been evolving together in symbiosis for so long that neither can now exist without the other.

In fact, it has been suggested that all animal and plant cells are actually the product of a symbiotic relationship, albeit one that began billions of years ago. Unlike simple bacteria cells, your cells contain a variety of organelles – compartments within the cell which perform particular tasks. One type of these, the mitochondria, are responsible for producing energy in a form that can be used by the molecular machinery of the cells. Animal metabolism is balanced on such a knife-edge that if you removed all mitochondria from your body, you would probably only have enough energy to last a few seconds. Cyanide, for example, blocks one of the crucial chemical pathways in energy production, rapidly bringing most metabolic processes to a halt.

Mitochondria are interesting because some of the information used to make them is encoded on DNA actually found in the mitochondria, rather than on the cell's main 'database' of DNA (the 23 pairs of chromosomes in humans). This has led to speculation that mitochondria were once separate organisms, like the non-organelle containing bacteria we find today. At some point fairly early on in life's history, the mitochondrial organisms began a symbiotic relationship with other cells, the end result of which was the integration of the mitochondria into the cells of all multi-cellular organisms.[28]

Reproduction versus caring

In species which care for their young by providing food and protection, a choice has to be made. A parent has only so much time and resources. It must decide how much of this should be expended in reproduction (generating new individuals), and how much should be spent caring for already existing young.[29] There will be a compromise solution: clearly spending all one's time caring and none of it actually reproducing is a poor strategy. Many organisms practise the reverse, concentrating on reproduction but spending no time caring for the new young. Most mammals opt for something in between, producing fewer offspring than they theoretically could, but making sure that these offspring are well looked after and thus have a good chance of surviving to reproductive age. The exact compromise reached will obviously depend on the species and the environmental conditions (e.g., available resources, risk of predation, etc.) that it finds itself in.

Such 'family planning' was in the past seen as an example of group selection. It was thought that animals regulated their offspring number so that the population did not get over-stretched – in other words, they were doing it for the good of the group. We can now see that there is a simpler, selfish explanation. Each individual wants to maximise its reproductive success. This isn't just measured in terms of number of offspring, however – if none of those offspring succeeds in reproducing, the parent's efforts have been worthless. Thus, as with kin selection, animals have to weigh up the costs, risks and benefits involved. Once again, we don't see chimps sitting down with calculators – instead, the 'solution' has been found by natural selection acting to favour genes which tend the animal's behaviour towards the 'correct' balance. Dawkins concludes the point:

[I]*ndividual parents practise family planning, but in the sense that they optimise their birth-rates rather than restrict them for public good. They try to maximise the number of surviving children that they have, and this means having neither too many babies nor too few. Genes that make an individual have too many babies tend not to persist in the gene pool, because children containing such genes tend not to survive to adulthood.*[30]

Battle of the sexes

Women are from Venus and men are from Mars. While numerous intellectuals have made efforts to argue that gender differences in humans are the result of social conditioning, differences in behaviour between the sexes persist throughout the animal kingdom. While the human nature/nurture debate is long and controversial, it seems unrealistic to propose that the differences between male and female behaviour observed in so many different species is the result of socialisation. I would argue that it is unrealistic to propose this for humans as well, but that's another story.

The essential reason for these differences is that, at least in most sexually reproducing species, males and females have very different priorities. The cost to a male of reproducing is small – he merely sheds a few million sperm. Given that the cost is small, it is obviously not worth the male expending much effort in caring for the offspring. Sure, the offspring may die as a result of his neglect, but he can always go off and find another female – he hasn't wasted much time and effort either way. In fact, his best policy may be to have as many offspring as possible by as many different females as possible, maximising his chances of success for a minimal expenditure of effort.

For females, however, the cost of reproduction is much larger. For a start, an egg is a much bigger investment than sperm, using up more resources and energy. In those species that incubate the fertilised egg internally, like mammals, the female also bears the mammoth cost of pregnancy. She cannot simply abandon her new offspring and go and have more – she has already invested too much time and energy in the production of the child simply to walk away. Thus, while we may not expect males to be particularly choosy about who they mate with, the female will want to ensure that she finds the right male. In particular, she will want to choose one who won't do a runner and who can be relied upon to help raise the children. Remember that from the genes' point of view, there is no reason for the male to help the female *per se*, or *vice versa* – they simply need each other to reproduce. Hence the famous 'battle of the sexes'.

In many species, however, both parents help care for the young. How are the females managing to coerce the males into this caring role, given that they would usually be far better off finding new mates? The answer is that females do have a large amount of power over males. They can refuse to mate with a male until he has 'proved his worth'. If all females 'screen' prospective mates in this way, a promiscuous male may find himself without a mate at all, and his genes will perish.

Hence the lengthy, costly and sometimes downright bizarre courtship rituals of which TV nature documentaries are so fond. Males are forced to undergo some sort of performance, intended to demonstrate their commitment to the female, before mating can begin. This performance may involve challenges which demonstrate the male's ability to be a good parent, such as feats of strength or the provision of food for the female (taking her out to dinner, as it were). Their content need not reflect actual ability, however – it is sufficient that they simply involve the male expending a great deal of time, as this is a 'cost' in reproduction. A male who has had to spend ages wooing a female is unlikely then to desert her, if he knows that he will have to start all over again with any other female.

Of course, this strategy is only successful if there aren't a large number of females who are prepared to forgo the courtship ritual and mate immediately. As with our population of Tit-for-Tattists, there will always be a small number of cheats on each side. There will be females who risk being deserted by not bothering with courtship, and there will be males who are unfaithful. The risky females do alright as long as most males are faithful – they will only rarely be exploited by promiscuous males. The unfaithful males do alright as long as there are a few females who do not bother putting them to the test.

This is an over-simplification, and the exact details will, of course, depend on the risks, benefits and costs involved. The point is that the extravagant displays and rituals seen in nature can be explained in terms of each individual acting selfishly, or rather in accordance with his or her selfish genes. Interestingly, while in most animal species it is the males that have brightly coloured appendages, feathers and so forth, in humans the roles seem to be reversed – it is women that wear the intricate garments and make-up, while the men all wear suspiciously similar suits. Whether or not this gives weight to the 'gender from social conditioning' argument is a matter for debate but, together with other oddities in humans' 'battle of the sexes', it led Dawkins to write the quotation with which I started this book.

What is a gene for?

This question is intentionally ambiguous. Do I mean what is the purpose of genes, or am I talking about the phenotypic effects of genes (as in a gene for blue eyes)? The answer is both. To start with the former, I hope it is now clear that genes have no 'purpose'. This teleological confusion has resulted from the apparently purposeful behaviour exhibited by many animals, which on a grander scale is reflected by the apparently purposeful nature of evolution – the fact that so many species appear to be designed for their environment. Natural selection shows us how such a system can come about through blind natural processes. Genes that create phenotypes well suited to exploiting their environments succeed, while their less well adapted peers perish. There is no purpose. Most animals that exhibit such 'purposeful' behaviour do not possess a nervous system complex enough to model the future in the way necessary for a sense of purpose. After all, the growth of plants looks like goal-orientated behaviour in time-lapse sequences (another favourite of nature documentaries). Instead, organisms are given 'hard-wired' rules by their genes, which over evolutionary time have been shown to be successful (as always, in the sense of increasing the chances of those genes making it through to the next generation). Of course, there is at least one species that does engage in truly purposeful behaviour as well – us. Maybe there are others, but certainly not many.

The second interpretation is more tricky, and

touches on the problems of genetic determinism and reductionism. Genetic determinism refers to the idea that an organism's phenotype, including its behavioural repertoire, is determined exclusively by its genes. It is stereotyped in tabloid language by the defence: 'It wasn't me, it was my genes!' Reductionism is similar, in that it argues that all evolutionary phenomena can be explained at the level of the gene (i.e., all explanations can be reduced to gene-based explanations).

The idea that genes

. . . are the only determining programme of all living things, [that] *what drives and determines life is the genetic imperative to survive and reproduce at the expense of everything else . . .*[31]

is clearly wrong, and although some people seem to think that Dawkins holds this view, neither he nor any other serious thinker does. If you lose a leg in a car accident, your genes have had nothing to do with it. Consequently, the contingencies of the environment are a major factor in determining the eventual fate of the individual. Furthermore, genes are not the sole cause of those phenotypes usually listed as 'genetically determined'. Consider our gene for blue eyes. What does this mean? It certainly doesn't mean that if we place the relevant length of DNA on a table it will miraculously construct a fully functional blue eye. It means that, in the presence of numerous other genes and cellular machinery, given the correct environmental conditions, the gene will produce a blue pigment, whereas another gene in the presence of the same collection of genes and cellular machinery, with the same environmental conditions, may produce a brown eye. This is a bit long-winded, so biologists usually just say 'a gene for blue eyes'.

No one factor, genetic or environmental, can be considered as the single 'cause' of any part of a baby. All parts of a baby have a near infinite number of antecedent causes. But a difference between one baby and another, for example a difference in length of leg, might easily be traced to one or a few simple antecedent differences, either in environment or in genes. It is differences that matter in the competitive struggle to survive; and it is genetically-controlled differences that matter in evolution.[32]

This explains why we can validly talk about genes for mate preference, altruism and so forth, even though these behaviours are obviously not contained within the single protein produced by the gene:

[T]o *speak of a gene 'for' something only ever means that a* change *in the gene causes a* change *in the something. A single genetic* difference, *by changing some detail of the molecules in cells, causes a* difference *in the already complex embryonic processes, and hence in, say, behaviour.*[33]

Once this idea has been grasped, the entire nature/nurture debate becomes far less black and white. No single characteristic of an individual can be said to be exclusively the product of genes – the environment is required to produce any characteristics at all. Similarly, no trait can simply be the product of nurture, since if there were no genes acting there would be nothing for nurture to work with! Even if you argue that all important aspects of human psychology result from learning and social conditioning (a point I disagree with), you still need genes to create a brain which is capable of learning and being conditioned in that way. This allows Dawkins to say:

[I]t is perfectly possible to hold that genes exert a statistical influence on human behaviour while at the same time believing that this influence on human behaviour can be modified, overridden or reversed by other influences.[34]

Furthermore, whether or not you are a determinist has nothing to do with genes. To be a determinist in the general sense simply means that you believe that all events, be they a rock falling down a hill or you deciding to watch TV, are predetermined by preceding physical events. Whether or not those preceding events have a genetic basis is irrelevant:

[W]hat difference can it possibly make whether some of those physical causes are genetic? Why *are genetic determinants thought to be any more ineluctable, or blame-absolving, than 'environmental' ones? The belief that genes are somehow super-deterministic, in comparison with environmental causes, is myth of extraordinary tenacity, and it can give rise to real emotional distress.*[35]

Admittedly, Dawkins' language in *The Selfish Gene* has probably helped to prolong this myth, but nothing in it follows from the principles of selfish gene theory.

What about reductionism? There are two issues at stake here. Firstly, can we successfully reduce all evolutionary explanation to the level of the gene? And, relatedly, does this mean that selection only operates at the level of the gene?

Reduction and levels of selection

The disagreement between evolutionary biologists usually focuses on the second of these questions. Many feel that Dawkins is asking selection to act exclusively on genes. While almost everyone agrees that much selection happens at the gene level, some argue that selective forces act on organisms, and possibly on groups as well. Some deny that genes can possibly have the causal power that Dawkins demands of them. In more technical language,

[T]*he claim is that, in some populations, properties of individual alleles are not positive causal factors in the survival and reproductive success of the relevant organisms.*[36]

The sort of example these critics point to is the problem of a gene whose effect is dependent on the frequency of other genes (or itself). Consider our Tit-for-Tat strategy earlier. Behaving in a Tit-for-Tat fashion is more profitable if everyone else is following the same strategy, or some similar strategy that will lead to mutual co-operation. If you are heavily outnumbered by cheats, however, it loses much of its appeal. If Tit-for-Tat behaviour sometimes increases survival and sometimes doesn't, then how can we say that there is a *causal* relation between that behaviour and survival? And if the behaviour doesn't cause survival, then how can a gene for that behaviour do so?

We have already uncovered the answer! Genes cannot act in isolation – their effects are always contingent upon the environment, and that environment includes other genes. Just as a piece of protein-encoding DNA won't produce an eye unless it has the correct environment (e.g., the environment of a developing embryo with a complete genome), so some genes will not produce benefits unless a reasonable number of other individuals share that gene.[37] The fact that in the first case the 'environmental genes' are in the same individual, while in the second they are in a different individual, is irrelevant – both are part of the gene's environment!

Another strategy, exemplified by Dawkins' most famous critic, Stephen Jay Gould, is to argue that, even if genes have causal effects on phenotypes, natural selection cannot act directly on genes, as they are tied up in bodies. Thus, phenotypes are selected, not genes:

According to Gould, Dawkins is unable to give genes 'direct visibility to natural selection'. Bodies must play intermediary roles in the process of selection, and, since the properties of genes do not map on one–one fashion onto the properties of bodies, we cannot attribute selective advantages to individual alleles.[38]

The properties of a gene in this sense means the thing that the gene is for, or determines (e.g., 'blue-eyeness'). We know that to say that a gene determines X means that it determines X *in the correct environment*, and we have seen that this environment includes other genes. More formally, we should say that a gene A determines X *relative to another gene B* in a certain environment, only if organisms which possess A and B show the characteristic X in that environment. A gene that stops eye production determines eye colour (in the sense of not having one!) relative to another gene for eye pigment, regardless of what the eye pigment gene is. Just because we say that a gene determines one characteristic doesn't mean that it can't determine another – our gene for no eye pigment is also a gene for no eye! Furthermore, the two 'properties' of the gene need not have the same influence on the organism's chances of survival. A gene for a particularly good immune system may make its carrier more susceptible to certain auto-immune diseases. If this gene is widespread in the population, however, we can be pretty sure that it has been selected because its benefits outweigh its costs, in evolutionary terms.

On a slight diversion, you may by now be feeling that the organism has been almost stripped of identity. An organism's environment includes the physical world and other individuals in it. The gene's environment includes the immediate physical environment (e.g., the organism's tissues) and other genes in that body, but it extends beyond the organism to the 'outside world', and even includes the genes of other organisms. The barrier of the individual is invisible to genes. Likewise, the effects of genes are not confined to the individuals that possess them – we can validly talk about genes for building beaver dams, because such genes (in the correct environment, etc., etc.) influence a behaviour that results in the animal (a beaver) building a dam. Dawkins has coined the phrase 'the extended phenotype' to describe this, because the gene's effects (its phenotype) 'extend' beyond the organism.

Returning to the main thread, we can see that just because genes affect the environment (be it internal or external to the organism) in complicated and indirect ways, we do not have to abandon the claim that there is a causal link between those genes and their effects, and thus a causal link between those genes and any selective advantage conferred by those effects. Organisms are vehicles; genes are replicators.

It can be argued nevertheless that there are times when it makes sense to talk about a trait in terms of the organism. Consider our beaver gene for dam building. Strictly speaking, this is a gene for beaver behaviour that leads to dam building. The behaviour is certainly a trait of the beaver. Is it not valid to describe it in these terms, and thus view selection at this level?

We are no longer asking which is the 'correct' level at which to view selection. We are asking whether there is a correct level at all. Causal stories can be described from several points of view. Dawkins' opinions on the subject shift somewhat between *The Selfish Gene* (1976) and *The Extended Phenotype* (1982). Dawkins initially implies, intentionally or not, that there is only one correct description of the causal process, and that this description always puts genes centre-stage. *The Extended Phenotype* seems to relax this view and argue instead that there are often alternative ways of looking at selection, but that the gene-centred view will always be as good (or better) than any others available. The argument for genic selection then becomes a pragmatic one. It is the only way of looking at the matter that is guaranteed to yield a correct causal story (although other ways – e.g., from the organism's point of view – may sometimes be as correct).

In one sense, which level or levels of selection are valid in any given circumstance depends on the empirical circumstances, as Elliot Sober points out:

There is no a priori reason to prefer lower-level selection hypotheses over higher ones. This preference is not a direct consequence of 'logic' or the scientific method.[39]

Selection will act on any entity that exists long enough for its frequency in the population to be changed – i.e., a replicator. In practice, it is difficult to see how something as unique and temporary as an individual, let alone a group, could qualify as a replicator. However, it is perfectly possible that genic selection will give rise to phenomena that *appear* to be a consequence of individual selection or group selection and, in some circumstances, it may be pragmatic to analyse selection as if it were acting at these levels.

An imperfect analogy is the workings of a car. You can choose, if you want, to explain a car's engine in terms of physical forces, particles, and their interactions. Such a fine-grained approach may be 'complete' in some causal sense, but you will probably find it next to useless. Alternatively, you can describe the car in engineering terms, naming the components of the engine and how they interact. Or you could apply a functional description, stating how those parts are controlled to produce a desired effect. There are many 'levels' of explanation.

Similarly, when the car crashes, you could

argue that the 'true' cause of the crash was the set of velocities, forces and so forth that described the system just prior to the accident. Or you could say that the driver failed to brake in time. Or that the road was wet. All of these conditions and descriptions are 'true' causes of the crash, yet some will matter more to physicists, others to tyre engineers, and others to lawyers.

So we can perhaps sympathise with Dawkins' denial of group and individual selection as providing 'true' causal stories, much as a physicist may deny that a failure to brake is the correct causal story. We can also see Gould's point, noting that it is useful in some circumstances to take a coarser-grained approach. But if we ask 'What does selection affect?', we are asking which entities change over evolutionary time because of selection – and these can only be genes:

For natural selection to adjust the frequency of something over the generations, the entity must have a sufficient degree of permanence. You cannot adjust the frequency of an entity between times t1 and t2 if between the two times the entity has ceased to exist . . . Natural selection cannot work on whole lions because lions die; they are not permanent. Nor can it work on the genome. The [. . .] lion's offspring inherit only genetic fragments, not a copy of a whole genome, from their parents.[40]

Evolution and natural selection

I have given only a brief introduction to the question of whether or not selection operates solely at the gene level. Unfortunately, the debate tends rapidly to suck in philosophical concepts like causality which are beyond the scope of this book. Even more unfortunately, people seem to get confused between questions about natural selection and questions about evolution. The question, 'Are genes the only level at which natural selection operates?' is logically distinct from 'Is natural selection the only driving force in evolution?'. While Dawkins may respond to the first with an emphatic 'yes', he answers 'no' to the second – after all, many events in evolution are simply bad (or good) luck:

Over the very long timescale, asteroids and other catastrophes bring evolution to a dead stop, major taxa [categories of organisms] *and entire radiations* [sets of taxa] *go extinct.*[41]

Any orthodox Darwinian would be entirely happy with major extinctions being largely a matter of luck.[42]

This sounds very similar to Gould's statement of pluralism, intended to be opposed to Dawkins' view:

[Pluralists] *accept natural selection as a paramount principle, but then argue that a set of additional laws, as well as a large role for history's unpredictable contingencies, must also be invoked to explain the basic patterns and regularities of the evolutionary pathways of life.*[43]

Surely two such great thinkers could not have been talking at cross-purposes all this time? The answer is no, of course not – but a large number of people who claim to endorse or represent the views of one or other of them have been doing so. Daniel Dennett's book *Darwin's Dangerous Idea* (1995), heavily and rightly criticised by Gould, is one example.

Gould's pluralism does not just include random lumps of rock hitting the earth, which of course all theories of evolution have to allow for. He also believes that some of the genetic change seen in species over time is not the product of natural selection. Gould argues that a large number of genetic mutations are evolutionarily 'neutral' in that they confer neither benefit nor handicap on the organism, and thus don't affect the frequency of the gene in the next generation. A population may 'drift' from one genetic make-up to another via a succession of such non-adaptive mutations.

Gould has suggested that the fact that the fossil record does not show a gradually changing population (as evolution by natural selection would imply), but instead a succession of discrete species, indicates that species-formation may be a sudden (and possibly non-adaptive) genetic event, such as a rapid reorganisation of the genome (e.g., a change in chromosome number).

The point I want to make here is not which of the two camps is right on these matters. It is a debate that will carry on for many years and, I believe, can only really be concluded by more empirical evidence, rather than theoretical reasoning. The real point is that Gould and Dawkins agree that natural selection is one of the most important forces in evolution, and they also agree that there are other forces at work. The more profound disagreement is over the level at which selection acts.

Values and facts

I conclude with my most important point, and the source of more misguided criticisms of *The Selfish Gene* than anything else. Many feel that Dawkins' theory somehow undermines morality, especially religious morality, by reducing all human behaviour to the level of 'selfish' genes. This assertion is based on two false premises. The first is that human behaviour is irrevocably decided by genes: genetic determinism. We have seen that this is false. Humans, more than any other species on the planet, have the capacity to 'rebel' against the interests of their genes, and in any case, a large part of human psychology results from cultural influences.

The second premise is that the statement 'X is natural' or 'X is an evolved tendency' somehow implies that 'X is right' or 'X is wrong'. Consider the following statements: 'It is natural to feel and act aggressively towards someone who has hurt you'; 'It is right to feel and act aggressively towards someone who has hurt you'. Do you think the truth or otherwise of the first statement holds any importance for the truth or otherwise of the second? Me neither. All we must allow is that, if we want humans to be moral creatures, we must turn against some of our natural urges. But it may well be right (if 'unnatural') to do so.

This works both ways, of course. Selfish gene theory, and evolution in general, may have a lot to say about the facts propagated by some religions, but it can say nothing about their moral systems (even when those religions claim, falsely, that their morals are based on facts – how can they be?). While Dawkins as a man does indeed disagree with many religions' stands on morality (he himself is a humanist), his theory says nothing about them. Perhaps many of Dawkins' critics will feel reassured by this.

Yet the critics are still there. Merryl Wyn Davies claims that:

Genes have become an alternative 'moral code', our only source of 'rules of conduct'.[44]

I am not sure to whom 'our' is supposed to refer here – clearly not Wyn Davies herself, certainly not me, nor Richard Dawkins. Perhaps authors who claim that this 'gene morality' is widespread could indicate some of its followers, so that we could all ridicule them. Wyn Davies goes on to say that:

Science that asserts . . . that we began as a 'genocidal species', is doing one of two things. Either it is reading the gross brutalities of the 20th century into our past, or producing theories that excuse the vileness of the present.[45]

The term 'genocidal species' already carries moral weight, so let us replace it with 'species with a tendency to kill one another when it was to their own individual advantage', as this is the closest to Davies' claim that an evolutionary biologist is likely to get. The 20th century has clearly got nothing to do with it – we are concerned with events that happened thousands, if not hundreds of thousands, of years ago. So we are left concluding that the actions of our ancestors aeons ago somehow carry moral weight in the present.

I suppose there is a sense in which the past justifies the present. After all, morality is built on tradition and precedent, and a sense of 'being right for all time'. It is the same thinking that leads landowners to bar access to their estate every so often, lest the pathways on it become public rights of way by default. In this case, surely, the fact that we judge our ancestors' actions as 'wrong' undermines our faith in morality?

Maybe it does, but we do it all the time. By today's standards, many – if not most – pre-20th-century societies were unjust and morally misled. We have no problem in criticising the actions of our ancestors who fought the Crusades – why do we have such trouble with ancestors thousands of years before that?

The response, of course, is that we share those genes that allegedly 'made' them a 'genocidal species'. So what? I share almost all of my genes with Adolf Hitler, as do you, yet I hope nobody would see this as a reason for categorising us as fascists.

Dawkins makes his point on the subject at the start of *The Selfish Gene*:

I am not advocating a morality based on evolution. I am saying how things have evolved. I am not saying how we humans morally ought to behave. I stress this, because I know I am in danger of being misunderstood by those people, all too numerous, who cannot distinguish a statement of belief in what is the case from an advocacy of what ought to be the case.[46]

Clearly, he didn't stress it enough.

Towards evolutionary psychology

Before wrapping the entire topic up, I can't resist a quick diversion to introduce readers to an area that I myself have spent some time thinking about. I said in the previous section that you cannot deduce moral values from scientific facts, and I stand by that. It is true, however, that science inevitably informs and influences moral debate, a point emphasised by Merryl Wyn Davies:

In society, where science wields and protects authority, scientific facts affect directly how moral and ethical questions are answered.[47]

Personally, I don't have a problem with this state of affairs. If a moral debate takes place in a factual vacuum, a great deal of time can be wasted arguing about solutions to a problem that simply wouldn't work. For example, if you object to State money being spent on AIDS victims because they must be homosexual (believe me, I've heard it), then you had better be ready to retract your 'solution' when I tell you that HIV is mostly transmitted through heterosexual sex. What I can't tell you to do, unfortunately, is retract your stance on homosexuality – that is a moral issue. Even if I could argue that homosexuality was natural, I would be no closer to proving that it was right. Similarly, arguing that homosexuality was unnatural would not show that it was wrong.

I also said that humans have the ability to turn against their 'selfish genes', and that much of our psychology is the result of cultural influences. This doesn't mean that our genes have *no* influence on our psychology. Furthermore, as we can change our culture but not our genes (well, not for the moment, anyway), it would be wise to understand the extent of genetic influences on human psychology before proposing any radical social change.

Evolutionary psychology seeks to do just this. It hopes to provide evolutionary explanations for some aspects of human psychology, in particular those aspects that seem to be universal. Some of these aspects are fairly uncontroversial. Most evolutionary biologists have no problem in accepting, for example, that human sexual desire is a product of natural selection. Most people call it 'natural' or 'part of being human'. Some of evolutionary psychology's theories have provoked outrage. As usual, much of the criticism is based on the 'you are saying humans are X, and we *want* humans to be Y, therefore you must be wrong' fallacy. I hope by now that you can see the problem in this argument.

Critics of evolutionary psychology will undoubtedly be delighted to hear that Dawkins is a firm supporter of the project. But I digress. I recommend Dylan Evans' *Introducing Evolutionary Psychology* for anyone who wants to pursue the subject.[48] To those dubious of the value of such a project, may I remind you that the human mind is extremely malleable and is largely shaped by culture. But if you are building a house, you want to know what starting materials are available, don't you?

Conclusion

Dawkins' theory of the selfish gene is a theory about replicators. It is a theory that applies under the following conditions:

1. There must be replicators – entities capable of producing copies of themselves.
2. A small error occurs when each copy is produced, leading to differences between the copies.

3. These differences affect the copying ability of
   the replicator.

That is pretty much it – whether the system is
played out on a computer simulation or over millions of years on earth, the principle is the same.
Replicators will be selected for their ability to
copy themselves, and will thus evolve ever more
complex ways of going about it. This may, but
need not, include the construction of complex
vehicles to house the replicators, and the
exploitation of other replicators' (or vehicles')
resources. It may also include co-operating with
other replicators, either in the same vehicle or in
another one.

Genes, lengths of DNA, are the replicators on
which all life (on earth, anyway) is based. They
have co-operated to build giant vehicles, organisms, of increasing complexity. We are such
organisms. They do not control us, however.
They have a more immediate control system to
ensure their survival – the brain. In humans, however, something quite extraordinary has happened. That brain has become so complex that it

can turn around and appreciate the replicators that have created it, and ignore the purpose for which they designed it.

Dawkins' theory, although it may well run into technical difficulties with some biologists and philosophers, has been widely misunderstood. Perhaps people have credited it with more theoretical power than it in fact has, seeing a monster where there is only a shadow. Undoubtedly, Dawkins' rhetoric has added to the confusion for some. I finish with a comment originally made by Andrew Brown in *The Guardian* in an article supposedly attacking Dawkins, but which Dawkins re-used in his subsequent reply:

It would be possible to write a long article demolishing almost everything people believe Richard Dawkins has said, using only his own words.[49]

Notes

1. Richard Dawkins, *The Selfish Gene*, Oxford: Oxford University Press, 1976, 1989 (rpt. 1999), p. 164. (All page references are to the 1989 edition, 1999 reprint.)

2. Merryl Wyn Davies, *Darwin and Fundamentalism*, Cambridge: Icon Books, 2000, p. 69. I should say from the outset that, although I believe Davies explicates many concepts superbly, I fear she may have misinterpreted Dawkins on several points.

3. 'You can't get an ought from an is.' The fact–value distinction stretches back to David Hume (1711–76), who, in the first section of *A Treatise of Human Nature*, Book 3 (1740), developed the idea that moral right and wrong cannot be derived from factual right and wrong: 'In every system of morality . . . I have always remarked, that the author proceeds for some time in the ordinary way of reasoning . . . when of a sudden I am surprised to find, that instead of the usual [proposition] *is*, I meet with no proposition that is not connected with an *ought*. This change is imperceptible; but is, however, of the last consequence. For as this *ought* . . . expresses some new relation of affirmation, it is necessary that it should be observed and explained; and at the same time that a reason should be given . . . how this new relation can be a deduction from others, which are entirely different from it.' There continues to be much debate about whether or

not moral judgements can be at least partly based on facts – a debate which, sadly, is too long to spell out here. It is sufficient for my purposes that we accept that 'it is *natural* to be selfish' does not inevitably lead to 'it is *right* to be selfish', and I hope most philosophers will be happy with this. A fuller explanation appears later in the book.

4. Wyn Davies, *Darwin and Fundamentalism*, op. cit.

5. Dawkins, *The Selfish Gene*, p. 1.

6. Ibid.

7. Ibid., pp. 264–6.

8. Ibid., p. 266.

9. Ibid., p. 33.

10. I say 'almost all' for two reasons. Firstly, some viruses use another molecule, RNA, to encode their genetic information. There was a long debate in biology about whether viruses should be counted as living things; all that the argument really showed was that there is no black-and-white definition of 'living'. How complicated must a reproducing molecule be, before it is considered alive? But I digress. The second reason is that arrogance should not let us preclude the possibility of life evolving on other planets. Dawkins and I both agree, I think, that although such life would come about by a process of evolution through natural selection, there is no reason to suppose that the replicators, or genes, involved should be composed of DNA.

11. Again, my proviso is to cover my back. Much of the

DNA in higher organisms does not encode proteins. This apparently junk DNA has recently become the focus of much study, as many believe that it serves important structural and regulatory roles for the genetic machinery. If this is true, then this DNA has, of course, been designed by natural selection just like its 'more functional' cousins. However, as it does not encode proteins, its effects will be limited to its immediate cellular environment.

12. As with most characteristics, eye pigment is in fact controlled by several genes, as several proteins are required to produce the necessary compounds. So how can I validly talk about a 'gene for blue eyes'? The essential point is that it is a gene for blue eyes, *all things being equal* – an issue examined in greater detail later.

13. Dawkins, *The Selfish Gene*, p. 28. See also G.C. Williams, *Adaptation and Natural Selection*, Princeton, NJ: Princeton University Press, 1966.

14. Mark Ridley, *Evolution*, Oxford: Blackwell Science, 1996 (2nd edition), chapter 12.

15. Ibid.

16. Dawkins, *The Selfish Gene*, p. 147.

17. Ibid., p. 93.

18. See William Hamilton's papers, 'The genetical evolution of social behaviour (I and II)', in *Journal of Theoretical Biology*, vol. 7, 1964, pp. 1–16 and 17–52, for a complete description of kin selection.

19. Dawkins, *The Selfish Gene*, p. 166.

20. Ibid., p. 168.

21. Actually, Tit-for-Tat strategies are not always the most successful, but the best performers are all variations on it (e.g., Tit-for-Two-Tat). Exactly which strategy will come out on top depends on the pay-offs involved, and which other strategies it is playing against. The matter is discussed at some length by Dawkins in chapter 12 of *The Selfish Gene*, which was added in the 1989 edition.

22. Note that for cheats to be detected – indeed, for repeated prisoners' dilemmas to work at all in a population of many animals – it is necessary that the animals be able to recognise each other as individuals. Thus, we should expect reciprocal altruism to be commonplace only in those species which can do this – and indeed, this is what is observed. Dawkins discusses the point with reference to vampire bats, which share their food (apparently with non-relatives), on p. 232 of *The Selfish Gene*.

23. Dawkins, *The Selfish Gene*, p. 69.

24. Ibid., p. 282.

25. Ibid., p. 217.

26. Ibid., p. 181.

27. Ibid.

28. Astute readers will realise that selfish gene theory should demand that the mitochondrial genes will retain their 'selfishness', and may thus engage in activities designed to increase their own propagation, even if it is at the expense of other genes in the organism. In fact, there is

some evidence that this is the case. Mitochondrial genes are passed only down maternal lines in many species, as no mitochondria from sperm enter the egg. Thus, mitochondrial genes should 'prefer' female offspring, as male offspring represent an evolutionary dead end. It seems that some mitochondrial genes do in fact bias the sex ratio in this way, though not in humans. Once again, this is a reminder that the organism is merely a vehicle, and that it is the genes that matter. (Examples of mitochondrial genes and a fuller explanation are given in Matt Ridley, *The Red Queen: Sex and the Evolution of Human Nature*, Harmondsworth: Penguin Books, 1993.)

29. Of course, I am not talking about conscious decisions being made by the organism (humans probably excepted). I simply mean that genes will evolve which tend the organism towards the optimal behaviour (in terms of reproductive success), whatever that optimal may be.

30. Dawkins, *The Selfish Gene*, p. 122.

31. Ibid., p. 37.

32. Ibid., p. 281.

33. Ibid., p. 331.

34. Ibid.

35. Richard Dawkins, *The Extended Phenotype*, Oxford: Oxford University Press, 1982 (rpt. 1992), p. 11.

36. Kim Sterelny and Philip Kitcher, 'The Return of the Gene', in *Journal of Philosophy*, vol. 85, no. 7, July 1988, pp. 339–61 (p. 341).

37. What is a reasonable number? This will depend on the benefits conferred by the gene, the frequency of other genes and the effect that frequency has on the benefits, and so on.

38. Sterelny and Kitcher, 'The Return of the Gene', p. 347.

39. Elliot Sober, *Philosophy of Biology*, Boulder, CO: Westview, 1993, p. 106.

40. Ridley, *Evolution*, chapter 12.

41. Richard Dawkins, 'Human Chauvinism', review of *Full House* by S.J. Gould, in *Evolution*, vol. 51, no. 3, June 1997.

42. Richard Dawkins, review of *Wonderful Life* by S.J. Gould, in *The Sunday Telegraph*, 25 February 1990.

43. Stephen Jay Gould, 'Evolution: The Pleasures of Pluralism', in *New York Review of Books*, 26 June 1997. See also Gould, 'Darwinian Fundamentalism', in *New York Review of Books*, 12 June 1997.

44. Wyn Davies, *Darwin and Fundamentalism*, p. 40.

45. Ibid., p. 68.

46. Dawkins, *The Selfish Gene*, p. 3.

47. Wyn Davies, *Darwin and Fundamentalism*, p. 70.

48. Dylan Evans, *Introducing Evolutionary Psychology*, Cambridge: Icon Books, 1999.

49. Andrew Brown, 'Feud for Thought', in *The Guardian*, 11 June 1997.

References

Richard Dawkins, *The Selfish Gene*, Oxford: Oxford University Press, 1976, 1989 (rpt. 1999).

Richard Dawkins, *The Extended Phenotype*, Oxford: Oxford University Press, 1982 (rpt. 1992).

Dylan Evans, *Introducing Evolutionary Psychology*, Cambridge: Icon Books, 1999.

Mark Ridley, *Evolution*, Oxford: Blackwell Science, 1996 (2nd edition).

Kim Sterelny and Philip Kitcher, 'The Return of the Gene', in *Journal of Philosophy*, vol. 85, no. 7, July 1988, pp. 339–61.

Merryl Wyn Davies, *Darwin and Fundamentalism*, Cambridge: Icon Books, 2000.

Acknowledgements

I would like to thank Prof Richard Dawkins for guiding me in my initial research, and Dr Dylan Evans for his suggestions and support. Thanks also to all those who provided sounding boards for my thoughts, notably Jan Evetts and Antoine Jeanson. I am also deeply grateful to everyone at Icon Books, especially Richard Appignanesi for his patience and assistance.